WHAT WOULD MY CAT SAY?

A guess on What Cats Really think of Humans

I am hungry. Again.
What would my cat say?

I've got a date.
What would my cat say?

I'm sleeping late.
What would my cat say?

I'm eating a lot.
What would my cat say?

I think I'm getting fat.
What would my cat say?

I feel like crying.
What would my cat say?

I'm drinking my fourth cup
of coffee.
What would my cat say?

I'm feeling sexy.
What would my cat say?

My partner doesn't like cats.
What would my cat say?

I forgot to feed her.
What would my cat say?

I've been trying out a lot of clothes.

What would my cat say?

I haven't taken a shower.
What would my cat say?

I snore.
What would my cat say?

I'm binging on my favorite TV drama -- alone with a lot of popcorn.
What would my cat say?

I'm having pizza again for dinner.

What would my cat say?

I haven't gotten out of the
house for a while.
What would my cat say?

I've got a pimple.
What would my cat say?

I'm checking someone out.
What would my cat say?

I'm using my hands to eat.
What would my cat say?

I'm having my sixth cup of coffee for the day.
What would my cat say?

I've been eating all day.
What would my cat say?

My bed is a mess.
What would my cat say?

I'm too busy to pet her.
What would my cat say?

I've been staring at that last slice of pizza.
What would my cat say?

I declared that I'm going on
a diet.
What would my cat say?

I keep on saying I'm too fat.
What would my cat say?

It's raining.
What would my cat say?

I brought someone home.
What would my cat say?

I burned the roast.
What would my cat say?

I'm drunk.
What would my cat say?

I'm wearing glasses for the
first time.
What would my cat say?

(Create your own scenario in
the next sheets.)

What would my cat say?

What would my cat say?

What would my cat say?

What would my cat say?

What would my cat say?

What would my cat say?

What would my cat say?

What would my cat say?

What would my cat say?

What would my cat say?

What would my cat say?

What would my cat say?

What would my cat say?

What would my cat say?

What would my cat say?

What would my cat say?

www.ingramcontent.com/pod-product-compliance
Lightning Source LLC
Chambersburg PA
CBHW071932120726
48001CB00005B/1944